for you and for many

for you and for many

CONTEMPORARY ADDITIONAL TEXTS
FOR CELEBRATING THE LORD'S SUPPER

nick FAWCETT

First published in 2004 by

KEVIN MAYHEW LTD
Buxhall, Stowmarket, Suffolk, IP14 3BW
E-mail: info@kevinmayhewltd.com

KINGSGATE PUBLISHING INC
1000 Pannell Street, Suite G, Columbia, MO 65201
E-mail: sales@kingsgatepublishing.com

9 8 7 6 5 4 3 2 1 0

ISBN 1 84417 194 9
Catalogue No 1500681

Cover design by Angela Selfe
Edited by Katherine Laidler
Typesetting by Louise Selfe
Printed in Great Britain

Contents

Introduction

To Stuart and Nikki Jenkins
gratefully remembering times shared together

Introduction

Take away some things and you wouldn't notice the difference; take away others and the results are unthinkable. Imagine toad-in-the-hole with no sausages, bread pudding without bread, or milkshake without milk! It would be a travesty. The same is true in worship. Some would positively welcome a service with no sermon! Others, not least irregular churchgoers, would feel more comfortable without an offering/collection. Others again would like to see an end to rambling prayers, dirge-like hymns or repetitive choruses. The thought, though, of taking away the Lord's Supper is unimaginable. It stands at the heart of worship, instituted by Christ himself, uniting us with countless generations across the centuries right back to the Apostles and that poignant final meal in the upper room.

The feast is like no other – a mere taste and sip – yet it is able to nourish as nothing else can begin to, feeding us deep within, nurturing faith, releasing grace, filling to overflowing. We may have shared it innumerable times before; it doesn't matter: the broken bread and poured-out wine continue to speak in a way that captures the heart and stirs the imagination.

Can anything new be added to this most powerful of sacraments? Of course not, but the riches it conveys need to be brought out afresh to every generation. This book is offered as a small contribution towards that end. Designed for those leading worship, it offers a comprehensive resource covering the various aspects of the Lord's Supper: words of invitation, acclamation and celebration; prayers of approach, praise, confession, thanksgiving, intercession and dismissal; Scripture sentences (my own paraphrase), offering assurance of forgiveness, bringing promise and encouragement, or reminding us of the institution of the Supper itself; and, finally, blessings for the close of worship. Numbered consecutively for ease of recall, the units can be used flexibly: selected from just certain sections or put together from each as seems appropriate. Where responses are provided these are set in bold.

No one can offer a definitive resource for the Lord's Supper, nor would it be possible or desirable to supersede the rich heritage or words, symbol and tradition handed down across the years, but if something in this book can help make clearer the wonder of God's love, so eloquently expressed through bread and wine, then it will have been well worth the writing.

NICK FAWCETT

Words of invitation

1

Whoever you are,
  this table is spread for *you*.
Whatever you have done,
  this table is spread for *you*.
Whatever your faults or fears,
  your faith or doubt,
  this table is spread for *you*.
Christ recognised our weakness, and was still ready to die.
He knew we deserve nothing,
  yet he gave all.
Whoever you are,
  wherever your journey may have taken you,
  this table is spread for *you*.

2

Come now to this sacred table,
  for Christ is here, ready to meet your need.
Come with your sorrow and find joy,
  with your faults and find forgiveness,
  with your regrets and find hope,
  with your fears and find strength.
Come, if life is dark and find light,
  if your heart is troubled and find peace,
  if your spirit is hungry and find nourishment.
Come, just as you are,
  and meet with the one who welcomes you in love,
  who waits to set you free and to bring you fullness of life.
You are here,
  he is here;
  offer your worship
  and receive all he longs to give you.

3

The table is prepared,
  the meal is ready,
  Jesus is here!
He offers us bread,
  food for the soul,
  nourishing,
  nurturing.

He offers us wine,
   refreshment in spirit,
   reviving,
   renewing,
   redeeming.

His body was broken so that we might be made whole.
His blood was shed so that life might flow within us.

The table is prepared,
   the meal is ready,
   Jesus is here!
Come now,
   and celebrate the feast.

4

We are not here as of right
   but by the grace of God.
We have not come to parade any virtue
   but to acknowledge our faults and seek forgiveness.
This table speaks not about what *we* may do
   but what Christ has done;
   not about *our* love for him
   but *his* for us.
Here is where sorrow brings joy,
   despair, hope,
   defeat, victory,
   and death, life –
   the *Lord's* Supper!
Come to him,
   as you are,
   and open your heart to all that shall yet be.

5

Come to me, said Jesus, all who are tired of carrying heavy burdens,
   and I will give you rest.
Come, all who are hungry,
   and I will give you bread of heaven.
Come, you who are thirsty,
   and I will give you living water.
His invitation is to you,

to me,
to everyone –
to all who search for meaning,
who yearn for peace,
who crave forgiveness,
who ache for new beginnings.
Come, says Jesus,
eat,
drink,
taste and see that the Lord is good –
do this, in remembrance of me.

6

'This is my body,' said Jesus, 'broken for you' –
and it looked like the end,
an admission of defeat,
a closing of the curtain.

'This is my blood, shed for you' –
and it appeared hopeless,
the shadows lengthening,
the day all but over.

But it wasn't,
for sorrow was turned to joy,
darkness to light,
defeat to victory,
death to life.

Where hope seemed destroyed, life was born again;
where hatred seemed the victor, love reigned supreme;
where evil seemed triumphant, God had the final word.

So, then, we remember,
yet look forward;
we feel sorrow,
yet rejoice;
we commemorate a crucified Saviour,
yet worship the risen Lord.

7

Are you conscious of need,
  burdened by guilt,
  troubled by failure,
  dismayed by weakness?
It's the sick who need a physician.
Come,
  and be healed.

Are you conscious of emptiness,
  yearning for fulfilment,
  searching for meaning,
  craving for peace?
It's the hungry who need food.
Come,
  and be satisfied.

Christ is here,
  his arms outstretched,
  hands that were nailed to the cross extended in welcome.
He offers you mercy, strength and guidance,
  renewal of body, mind and spirit,
  a love that will never let you go
  and life everlasting.

Draw near,
  all who would taste his joy,
  know his care,
  rejoice in his wholeness
  and accept his grace.
Come now,
  and receive.

8

The table is prepared,
  the meal is ready:
  Jesus is here!

He offers you bread,
  food for your soul,
  nourishing and satisfying.

He offers you wine,
   refreshment for your spirit,
   reviving and renewing.

His body was broken so that we might be made whole.
His blood was shed so that new life might flow within us.

The table is prepared,
   the meal is ready:
   Jesus is here!

Come now,
   and celebrate.

9

Are you searching for meaning?
The table is laid.
Are you yearning for acceptance?
The invitation is for all.
Are you burdened by guilt?
Christ died for you.
Are you looking for hope?
The Lord is here.
Are you hungry and thirsty, longing for succour?
Come now,
   eat,
   drink,
   and find nourishment for your souls,
   food to satisfy,
   now and always.

10

Bring your heartache, bring your tears,
   bring your worries, stress and fears.
Bring your troubles, hurt and care,
   bring your doubt, dismay, despair.
Bring your weakness, bring your shame,
   bring your faults and sense of blame.
Bring your aching deep inside,
   all the emptiness you hide.
Bring your all, lay bare your soul,
   Christ is here to make you whole.

11
His body was broken,
  not for the few,
  the special,
  the elite,
  but for you
  and for many.

His blood was shed,
  not for the perfect,
  the righteous,
  the holy,
  but for you
  and for many.

Draw near, then, with faith.
Eat and drink,
  whoever you are.
Christ offered his life
  and offers his love,
  for you,
  for many,
  for all.

12
Does life bring confusion,
  a string of questions that baffle and bemuse?
Remember that Jesus in Gethsemane wrestled with the bleakness of doubt.

Does life bring sadness,
  anguish and hurt deep within?
Remember that Jesus in Gethsemane wrestled with the bleakness of sorrow.

Does life bring pain,
  testing your endurance to the limit and beyond?
Remember that Jesus on the cross wrestled with the bleakness of suffering.

Does life bring despair,
  a sense of being abandoned, hopelessly alone?
Remember that Jesus on the cross wrestled with the bleakness of isolation.

Whatever life brings,
  whatever you may face,
  remember that this table speaks not of easy answers

but of the God who understands our questions,
   endures our sorrow,
   shares our suffering
   and knows what it is to feel alone.
Faith offers no immunity from life's ills,
   no guarantees of earthly blessing,
   but in bread and wine we are reminded that, whatever may disquiet
      and destroy,
   we will find sunshine after storm,
   laughter after tears,
   light after darkness,
   life after death.

Christ was broken.
He has risen.
He will come again,
   and finally there will be an end to all that denies his love
   and frustrates his will.
Until then,
   hold fast,
   keep faith,
   and hope in the Lord.

Prayers of approach

13
Gracious God,
   weak, wilful and worthless, we come to you nonetheless,
   knowing that you welcome us,
   and wait, every moment of every day,
   to bless us.
Faithless, foolish but thankful, we come . . .
   to be fed,
   to be filled.
Amen.

14
Not because we deserve your grace
   but because we desire your mercy,
   Lord,
   we come.

Not because we merit your goodness
   but because we need your love,
   Lord,
   we come.

Not because we can earn your blessing
   but because we yearn to be blessed,
   Lord,
   we come.

Not because we are faithful
   but because we are faithless,
   Lord,
   we come.

Not because we *have* to
   but because we *want* to,
   Lord,
   we come.

In response to your gentle, generous invitation,
   Lord,
   we come.
Amen.

15
Loving God,
    we rejoice that, though we consider ourselves unlovely,
    you consider us precious;
    though we deserve so little,
    you delight to give us so much;
    though we count ourselves sinners,
    you value us as children;
    though our faith is weak
    your love is strong.
So we come,
    assured of your grace,
    assured of your goodness,
    assured of your welcome,
    through Jesus Christ our Lord.
Amen.

16
Here at this table, Lord,
    through bread and wine,
    we would meet you and greet you,
    love you and serve you.

Here in this church, Lord,
    through our work and witness,
    we would meet you and greet you,
    love you and serve you.

Here in this world, Lord,
    through word and deed,
    we would meet you and greet you,
    love you and serve you.

Here on this day, Lord,
    in praise and worship,
    we would meet you and greet you,
    love you and serve you.

Here and everywhere, Lord,
    in life and in death,
    we would meet you and greet you,
    love you and serve you.

Lord Jesus Christ,
   draw near to us,
   as we draw near to you,
   and accompany us on our way.
Amen.

17
Lord Jesus Christ,
   we gather here,
   not at your command
   but at your invitation;
   not as servants
   but as friends;
   not out of duty
   but in grateful response.
We come in memory
   but also in joyful celebration;
   solemnly remembering the past
   but also jubilantly anticipating the future.
We come then in faith,
   asking that, through touching this moment,
   you will touch every moment
   with your gracious love
   and living presence.
Amen.

18
Lord Jesus Christ,
   as you requested
   so we come,
   in memory of you.
Grant that, as we eat and drink together,
   we may also welcome you into our hearts
   and receive you into our lives,
   so that we may remember you in the best way possible,
   honouring you in word and deed,
   and offering faithful service in your name.
Amen.

19

We come to this table, Lord, bringing our hunger –
    our need for help and strength,
    love and acceptance,
    wholeness and healing.

We come bringing our thirst –
    our longing for meaning and purpose,
    faith and understanding,
    pardon and renewal.

We come knowing we are empty
    and that you alone can fill us;
    knowing that our lives are parched
    and that you alone offer the water of life.

Feed,
    fill,
    nurture
    and nourish us,
    by your grace.
Amen.

20

Loving God,
    no words can express the wonder of your love,
    the extent of your goodness,
    the magnitude of your grace
    or the breadth of your saving purpose in Christ.
We thank you that this table says it all,
    speaking so simply,
    yet so eloquently,
    of how much you care for us,
    how much you have done for us,
    and how much you will yet do.
So we come,
    to receive from your hands
    and to give you our joyful worship in return,
    through Jesus Christ our Lord.
Amen.

Prayers of praise

21
Gracious God,
  you love us so much that you suffered for us in Christ,
  through his death offering forgiveness to all.
It is too much –
  words fail us!
In silence we worship you.

Silence

Living God,
  you love us so much that you won the victory for us in Christ,
  through his death bringing life to all.
It is too much –
  words fail us!
In silence we worship you.

Silence

Loving God,
  you love us so much that you come to us each day in Christ,
  feeding, nurturing and rekindling our faith.
It is too much –
  words fail us!
In silence we worship you.

Silence

Sovereign God,
  you love us so much that you are with us now,
  here in bread and wine,
  in prayer and worship,
  in the fellowship we share with you and one another.
It is too much –
  words fail us!
In silence we worship you.

Silence

To you, Lord God, be praise and glory.
Amen.

22
God of love,
>we acknowledge with wonder that you entered our world,
>taking on flesh and blood,
>sharing our humanity,
>your devotion so great
>that you identified yourself fully with us all,
>determined to redeem and restore.

Lord of all,
>**to you be praise and glory.**

God of grace,
>we marvel that you shared not just our life but our death,
>enduring the turmoil of Gethsemane,
>the humiliation of your trial and interrogation,
>the pain of flogging and thorns twisted into your head,
>the agony and isolation of the cross,
>suffering not just physical torment but spiritual desolation
>as you took on our sinfulness and wiped the slate clean.

Lord of all,
>**to you be praise and glory.**

God of power,
>we rejoice in your victory over death,
>your triumph over evil,
>your conquering of all that keeps us from you;
>bringing hope out of despair,
>faith out of doubt,
>and joy out of sorrow.

Lord of all,
>**to you be praise and glory.**

God eternal,
>we look forward to that day when your will shall be done,
>your purpose fulfilled
>and your victory complete;
>a day when your kingdom will be established
>and your blessings poured out for evermore.

Lord of all,
>**to you be praise and glory.**
>**Amen.**

23
Mighty God,
    we would praise you with our lips,
    declaring your greatness in word and song,
    for you are sovereign over all,
    the source of our being and goal of our striving,
    the Lord of heaven and earth,
    of all that is, and has been and shall be.
We come with joy.
We come in worship.

Majestic God,
    we would praise you in our minds,
    declaring your greatness in all we think,
    for you are ever at work,
    active in our world,
    involved in our lives,
    present in myriad ways around us;
    the Lord of all.
We come with joy.
We come in worship.

Marvellous God,
    we would praise you from our hearts,
    declaring your greatness in all we feel,
    for you are a gracious God,
    loving, forgiving, compassionate, caring,
    always there to strengthen and sustain,
    to equip and enable.
We come with joy.
We come in worship.

Matchless God,
    we would praise you in our lives,
    declaring your greatness in all we do,
    for to love you is to serve you,
    to know you is to work for your kingdom,
    to honour you is to respond to others,
    to revere your name is to respect your will.
We come with joy.
We come in worship.

Magnificent and monumental God,
    we *do* praise you, here and now,
    declaring your greatness with body, mind and soul,

for in bread and wine you welcome us again,
you bless us again,
you feed us again,
and you send us out once more to live and work for you.
We come with joy.
We come in worship.

In the name of Christ.
Amen.

24
Sovereign God,
you speak here,
at this table,
of your purpose:
your resolve to put an end, once and for all, to evil,
to establish a kingdom of peace and eternal blessing
where we will meet you face to face,
know you, even as we are known,
and rejoice in the light of your presence for evermore.
With awe and exultation,
we praise you.

Father God,
you speak here,
at this table,
of your love:
your devotion to all you have made,
your care for every one of us,
reaching out day after day
to support and encourage,
guide and equip,
comfort and reassure,
enthral and embrace.
With awe and exultation,
we praise you.

Merciful God,
you speak here,
at this table,
of your grace:
your acceptance of us as we are,
your willingness to forgive and go on forgiving,
your nature being always to have mercy,

despite the feebleness of our faith,
the paucity of our commitment
the half-heartedness of our service
and our repeated wilful disobedience.
With awe and exultation,
we praise you.

Great and marvellous God,
you speak here,
at this table,
to us all:
whatever our situation,
whatever our faults,
whatever our fears,
whatever our needs,
you are here,
arms outstretched,
bidding us welcome,
offering us life.
With awe and exultation,
we praise you.
Amen.

25
For all the ways good conquers evil,
Lord, we praise you.

For all the ways love conquers hate,
Lord, we praise you.

For all the ways joy conquers sorrow,
Lord, we praise you.

For all the ways faith conquers doubt,
Lord, we praise you.

For all the ways peace conquers war,
Lord, we praise you.

For all the ways hope conquers despair,
Lord, we praise you.

For all the ways trust conquers fear,
Lord, we praise you.

For all the ways truth conquers falsehood,
   Lord, we praise you.

For all the ways humility conquers pride,
   Lord, we praise you.

For all the ways mercy conquers vengeance,
   Lord, we praise you.

For all the ways life conquers death,
   Lord, we praise you.

For all the reasons we have
   to rejoice,
   to worship
   and to exult,
   Lord, we praise you.
Amen.

26
Lord Jesus Christ,
   as we recall how you broke bread and poured out wine,
   so we remember also your dealings with us across the years:
   the way you loved us before we even knew you,
   called us to be your disciples,
   cleansed us by your grace,
   and nurtured us, day after day, by your love.
Gracious Saviour,
   the same yesterday, today and tomorrow,
   receive our praise.

Lord Jesus Christ,
   as we look forward to our promised meeting with you face to face,
   and sharing with you in your Father's kingdom,
   so we look forward to all you will yet do in our lives:
   the faith to be deepened,
   the fellowship to share,
   the service to offer
   and the experiences still to unfold.
Gracious Saviour,
   the same yesterday, today and tomorrow,
   receive our praise.

Lord Jesus Christ,
    as we eat and drink together, sharing bread and wine,
    we recognise you are here now,
    speaking your word,
    displaying your love,
    nourishing our souls,
    and imparting life in all its fullness.
Gracious Saviour,
    the same yesterday, today and tomorrow,
    receive our praise.

For this table and all it represents,
    and for its testimony that eternity itself is in your hands –
    nowhere and no one beyond your grace,
    nothing in heaven or on earth able to separate us from your love –
    Lord, we bring you our joyful worship
    and heartfelt adoration,
    celebrating this feast with thanksgiving.
Gracious Saviour,
    the same yesterday, today and tomorrow,
    receive our praise.

In your name we ask it.
Amen.

27
Lord Jesus Christ,
    you suffered torment of mind
    to bring us peace.
With thankful hearts,
    we praise you.

You suffered agony of body
    to bring us healing.
With thankful hearts,
    we praise you.

You suffered hatred and hostility
    to bring us love.
With thankful hearts,
    we praise you.

You suffered the darkness of despair
    to bring us light.
With thankful hearts,
    we praise you.

You suffered the weight of our sin
   to bring us forgiveness.
With thankful hearts,
   we praise you.

You suffered the brokenness of the cross
   to make us whole.
With thankful hearts,
   we praise you.

You suffered death itself
   to bring us life.
With thankful hearts,
   we praise you.

Lord Jesus Christ,
   you help us to make sense of life in this imperfect unbalanced world,
   transforming the ugly into something beautiful,
   the awful into something awesome.
With thankful hearts,
   we praise you.
Amen.

28
Searching for meaning,
   hungry for truth,
     we meet you here, Lord,
     in bread and wine.
Gladly, we praise you.

Dismayed at weakness,
   frustrated by failure,
     we meet you here, Lord,
     in bread and wine.
Gladly, we praise you.

Burdened by shame,
   crushed by guilt,
     we meet you here, Lord,
     in bread and wine.
Gladly, we praise you.

Bemused by questions,
   troubled by doubts,

we meet you here, Lord,
   in bread and wine.
Gladly, we praise you.

Longing for peace,
   craving fulfilment,
   we meet you here, Lord,
   in bread and wine.
Gladly, we praise you.

Requesting refreshment,
   seeking renewal,
   we meet you here, Lord,
   in bread and wine.
Gladly, we praise you.

Yearning to follow,
   eager to serve,
   we meet you here, Lord,
   in bread and wine.
Gladly, we praise you.

Embraced by love,
   enveloped by grace,
   we meet you here, Lord,
   in bread and wine.
Gladly, we praise you.

Offering our worship,
   bringing our lives,
   we meet you here, Lord,
   in bread and wine.
Gladly, we praise you.

Receive, Lord, our joyful heartfelt worship.
Amen.

29
God of all,
   for your creative power,
   shaping the heavens and the earth,
   creating humankind in your image,
   fashioning a world of infinite beauty and variety,
   we give you our praise.
Receive our worship.

For your loving power,
    leading your people throughout history,
    guiding us in daily life,
    reaching out to help, provide and bless,
    we give you our praise.
Receive our worship.

For your redeeming power,
    always looking to forgive,
    always eager to restore,
    always able to help us start again,
    we give you our praise.
Receive our worship.

For your transforming power,
    bringing hope from despair,
    joy from sorrow,
    life from death,
    we give you our praise.
Receive our worship.

For your gentle power,
    made perfect in weakness,
    inviting rather than coercing,
    exemplified on the cross,
    we give you our praise.
Receive our worship.

For your victorious power,
    expressed through an empty tomb,
    understood in bread and wine,
    experienced through your living presence,
    we give you our praise.
Receive our worship.

Sovereign God,
    servant God,
    suffering God,
    saving God,
    for all you have done
    and continue to do in Christ,
    we give you our praise.
Receive our worship.
Amen.

30
Almighty God,
   enthroned in splendour,
   exalted over all,
   holy,
   righteous,
   wholly other,
   you are greater than we can ever imagine,
   mighty and mysterious,
   sovereign and supreme,
   beyond comparison or comprehension.
We come in awe.
We come in worship.
Glory and honour are yours, O Lord.

All-loving God,
   revealed in Christ,
   the Word made flesh,
   loving,
   forgiving,
   full of tenderness,
   you are nearer than we can ever imagine,
   caring and compassionate,
   gentle and generous,
   beyond all others in grace and goodness.
We come in awe.
We come in worship.
Glory and honour are yours, O Lord.

All-faithful God,
   at work through your Spirit,
   burning within us,
   empowering,
   equipping,
   enriching faith,
   you are stronger than we can ever imagine,
   supporting and strengthening,
   instructing and inspiring,
   beyond containment or constraint.
We come in awe.
We come in worship.
Glory and honour are yours, O Lord.

Almighty,
   all-loving,
   all-faithful God,
   we gather to share bread and wine,
   reminded afresh of your purpose,
   your promise
   and your presence,
   so wonderfully displayed in Christ,
   your Son,
   our Saviour.
We come in awe.
We come in worship.
Glory and honour are yours, O Lord.
Amen.

Prayers of confession

31
Lord Jesus Christ,
   in the things we have thought, we have failed you:
   judgemental, demeaning and unworthy thoughts
   that have frustrated your will
   and denied your grace.
Merciful Saviour,
   forgive us.

In the things we have said, we have failed you:
   harsh, thoughtless and foolish words
   that have frustrated your purpose
   and denied your love.
Merciful Saviour,
   forgive us.

In the things we have done, we have failed you:
   petty, selfish and dishonest actions
   that have frustrated your aims
   and denied your kingdom.
Merciful Saviour,
   forgive us.

In the things we have *not* thought,
   not said
   and *not* done
   we have failed you:
   concern unfelt,
   love unarticulated,
   compassion unexpressed;
   so many ways in which we have frustrated your Spirit
   and denied your renewing, redeeming power.
Merciful Saviour,
   forgive us.

Lord Jesus Christ,
   direct our thoughts, words and deeds,
   so that our lives may echo your goodness
   and redound to your praise.
Amen.

32

Foolish and faithless,
   we have wounded our loved ones, Lord,
   speaking harshly,
   acting selfishly,
   thinking unkindly
   and dealing falsely.
Lord Jesus Christ,
   Servant of all,
   for our failure to love,
   forgive us.

Foolish and faithless,
   we have wounded others, Lord,
   turning our back on suffering,
   insensitive to need,
   careless in word
   and thoughtless in deed.
Lord Jesus Christ,
   Servant of all,
   for our failure to love,
   forgive us.

Foolish and faithless,
   we have wounded ourselves, Lord,
   denying ourselves peace,
   saddling ourselves with guilt,
   rejecting your love
   and frittering away your gift of life.
Lord Jesus Christ,
   Servant of all,
   for our failure to love,
   forgive us.

Foolish and faithless,
   we have wounded you, Lord,
   ignoring your word,
   betraying your call,
   flouting your will
   and frustrating your kingdom.
Lord Jesus Christ,
   Servant of all,
   for our failure to love,
   forgive us.

Living Lord,
   in your mercy, make us whole,
   tend our wounds
   and heal the scars we have caused.
Live in us
   that we might live for you,
   to the glory of your name.
Amen.

33
Lord Jesus Christ,
   we look at you,
   we look at us,
   and the gulf is so wide,
   the difference so vast.
We turn aside in shame.
Have mercy.

We reflect on your words,
   we reflect on our deeds,
   and they seem poles apart,
   so little in us speaking of you.
We turn aside in shame.
Have mercy.

We think of your love,
   we think of our selfishness,
   and the contrast is so stark,
   the discrepancy so plain.
We turn aside in shame.
Have mercy.

We acknowledge your truth,
   we acknowledge our falseness,
   and the two seem completely opposed,
   no way the gap can be bridged.
We turn aside in shame.
Have mercy.

We consider your grace,
   we consider our sinfulness,
   the one so awesome,
   the other so awful.
We turn aside in shame.
Have mercy.

We eat bread,
    we drink wine,
    and the chasm is spanned,
    the divide at an end.
We turn aside in wonder.
For you have shown mercy, beyond our deserving.

Receive our joyful worship and grateful praise,
    offered in your name.
Amen.

34

Conscious of failure,
    ashamed of our weakness,
    living God, we come before you,
    having no claim on your love,
    no reason for deserving mercy,
    but trusting solely in your grace.
We are foolish and faithless.
Lord, forgive.

Conscious of our failure to love one another,
    we ask your pardon,
    for we have been thoughtless,
    self-centred,
    petty
    and judgemental,
    forgetful of the fellowship you call us to share together,
    of the bond that unites us in Christ.
We are foolish and faithless.
Lord, forgive.

Conscious of our failure to love our neighbour,
    we ask your pardon,
    for we have been mean,
    greedy,
    uncaring,
    insular,
    oblivious to need
    and unmoved by suffering.
We are foolish and faithless.
Lord, forgive.

Conscious of our failure to love ourselves,
  we ask your pardon,
  for we have struggled with a burden of guilt,
  denied ourselves the fullness of life you offer,
  pushing aside home truths we would rather not face
  rather than finding wholeness through facing them with you.
We are foolish and faithless.
Lord, forgive.

Conscious of our failure to love *you*,
  we ask your pardon,
  for we have been poor in discipleship,
  careless in devotion,
  lax in obedience
  and lacking in faith,
  our protestations of devotion belied by apathy,
  our talk of commitment denied by our deeds.
We are foolish and faithless.
Lord, forgive.

In so much we have failed you,
  and we know well enough we will fail you again . . .
  and again . . .
  but we know also that your grace will continue and your love endure,
  not just today
  but tomorrow,
  the next day,
  and for evermore.
To you, living God,
  be praise and worship,
  thanksgiving and adoration,
  now and always.
Amen.

35
Lord Jesus Christ,
  at this table we are reminded that you died for all,
  not just for us;
  that you love the world,
  not just the Church;
  your grace knowing no bounds,
  irrepressible,
  unquenchable.
For the narrowness of our vision,
  Lord, forgive us.

At this table we are reminded that you died for the sinful,
    not just the righteous;
    for the weak,
    not just the strong;
    your grace knowing no bounds,
    abundant,
    overflowing.
For the narrowness of our vision,
    Lord, forgive us.

At this table we are reminded that you died for the confused,
    not just the certain;
    for doubters,
    not just the assured;
    your grace knowing no bounds,
    free,
    unfailing.
For the narrowness of our vision,
    Lord, forgive us.

At this table we are reminded that you died for the hostile,
    not just those who love you;
    for those who reject your love,
    not just the committed;
    your grace knowing no bounds,
    unending,
    inexhaustible.
For the narrowness of our vision,
    Lord, forgive us.

As we eat and drink,
    broaden our horizons,
    enlarge our understanding,
    so that we may discern more fully all you have done for us
    and all you would do for others.
So may we receive
    and respond in loving service,
    to the glory of your name,
    through Jesus Christ our Lord.
Amen.

36

Jesus Christ,
Saviour and Redeemer,
in shame we make our confession.

You offer so much,
though we deserve so little.
Gracious Lord,
have mercy.

You give so freely,
we give back so grudgingly.
Gracious Lord,
have mercy.

Your grace is so rich,
our response so poor.
Gracious Lord,
have mercy.

You bless us so often,
we thank you so rarely.
Gracious Lord,
have mercy.

Your goodness is so sure,
our commitment so hesitant.
Gracious Lord,
have mercy.

Your pardon is so total,
our repentance so incomplete.
Gracious Lord,
have mercy.

Your love is so faithful,
our discipleship so faithless.
Gracious Lord,
have mercy.

Jesus Christ,
forgive us our many faults
and deliver us from all our weaknesses,
so that we might live more fully as your people.
Gracious Lord,
have mercy.
Amen.

37
Saviour Christ,
    you call us to follow you,
    but so often we go astray.
Lord of life,
    forgive us.

You call us to serve others,
    but instead we serve self.
Lord of life,
    forgive us.

You call us to love our neighbour,
    but we have turned our backs on need.
Lord of life,
    forgive us.

You call us to forgive,
    but foolishly we nurse grievances.
Lord of life,
    forgive us.

You call us to trust,
    but repeatedly we doubt.
Lord of life,
    forgive us.

You call us to speak of your love,
    but too often we stay silent.
Lord of life,
    forgive us.

You call us to take up our cross,
    but we are afraid of what that might cost.
Lord of life,
    forgive us.

You call us to remember all you have done,
    but so easily we forget.
Lord of life,
    forgive us.

Day after day, through what we do or fail to do,
    we betray your call and deny your love.
Lord of life,
    forgive us.

By your grace we ask it.
Amen.

38

Lord Jesus Christ,
   betrayed by one of your chosen twelve,
   we are conscious that we too,
   in our own way,
   betray you,
   preferring to serve our own interests rather than yours,
   compromising our convictions for the sake of instant satisfaction,
   selling out on our principles when temptation beckons.
We have been false and faithless.
Forgive us.

Lord Jesus Christ,
   denied by one who professed undying loyalty,
   we are conscious that, too often,
   for all our talk of commitment,
   we also have denied you,
   through our words when loyalty has threatened to prove costly,
   but most of all through our deeds,
   time and again what we say negated by what we do and who we are.
We have been false and faithless.
Forgive us.

Lord Jesus Christ,
   abandoned by those who once followed you,
   we are conscious that,
   so easily,
   we in our turn abandon you,
   backing off when faith makes demands,
   running away from what we would rather not face,
   or simply drifting away from your side.
We have been false and faithless.
Forgive us.

Lord Jesus Christ,
   nailed to a cross,
   bearing the sin of the world,
   we are conscious that *our* wrongdoing,
   as much as anyone's,
   contributed to your pain,
   driving the thorns into your head,
   the nails into your flesh,
   and the spear into your side.
We have been false and faithless.
Forgive us.

We come in need before you, Lord,
 for we have sinned,
 failing you in so much.
By your grace,
 pardon all that is past,
 and equip us to serve you better in the days ahead,
 as true to you as you are true to us.
We have been false and faithless.
Forgive us.
Amen.

39
Gracious God,
 in Christ you offer forgiveness,
 the past put behind us,
 mistakes forgotten,
 the slate wiped clean,
 yet we cannot quite believe it.
We are still troubled by guilt,
 and still turn over in our minds errors committed,
 misjudgements made
 and wrongs done.
For squandering your precious gifts,
 Lord, have mercy.

Gracious God,
 in Christ you offer hope,
 the future rich with promise,
 secure in your hands,
 assured for all eternity,
 yet we cannot quite believe it.
We still fret over what tomorrow might bring,
 and are still haunted by untold fears,
 unnamed possibilities
 and the unmentionable spectre of death.
For squandering your precious gifts,
 Lord, have mercy.

Gracious God,
 in Christ you offer fulfilment,
 the present offering a taste of your kingdom,
 life full to overflowing,
 each day transformed by your love,

yet we cannot quite believe it.
We still question our ability to get by,
    and still struggle along in our own strength,
    turned in on ourselves,
    wrapped up in our own small world.
For squandering your precious gifts,
    Lord, have mercy.

Gracious God,
    at this table remind us that in Jesus Christ,
    the same yesterday, today and tomorrow,
    you have absolved what is past,
    shaped what is to come,
    and consecrated this and every moment.
So may we celebrate your precious gifts,
    and share them with others,
    to your glory.
Amen.

40

Loving God,
    you have forgiven us so much,
    your nature always to have mercy
    despite our repeated disobedience to your will.
Pardon our failure to forgive in turn,
    our dwelling on past mistakes,
    our brooding over slights, imagined or otherwise,
    our raking up of old coals
    and our throwing them back in people's faces
    when they imagined them finally extinguished.
Help us not only to pray,
    but also to mean,
    forgive us our sins,
    as we forgive those who sin against us.

We have nursed grievances,
    looking to get our own back,
    to hurt as we have been hurt,
    to inflict our own brand of punishment.
Have mercy, Lord.
Help us not only to pray,
    but also to mean,
    forgive us our sins,
    as we forgive those who sin against us.

We have kept a score of wrongs,
 refusing to let go,
 allowing them to fester within,
 poisoning our relationships and ultimately us too.
Have mercy, Lord.
Help us not only to pray,
 but also to mean,
 forgive us our sins,
 as we forgive those who sin against us.

We have magnified errors out of all proportion,
 becoming carping and critical,
 seeing the faults of others
 while being blind to our own.
Have mercy, Lord.
Help us not only to pray,
 but also to mean,
 forgive us our sins,
 as we forgive those who sin against us.

We have refused to make allowances,
 declining to hear another's point of view,
 to try to understand,
 to deal with others as we would expect them to deal with us.
Have mercy, Lord.
Help us not only to pray,
 but also to mean,
 forgive us our sins,
 as we forgive those who sin against us.

Loving God,
 we warm to your promise of forgiveness,
 but we are so slow to forgive in turn.
Take from us narrowness of mind,
 bitterness of heart
 and meanness of spirit
 so that your unfailing mercy may flow as much *through* us as *to* us.
Help us not only to pray,
 but also to mean,
 forgive us our sins,
 as we forgive those who sin against us.

In Christ's name we ask it.
Amen.

41
Gracious God,
   there is so much wrong in our lives,
   so much that grieves and frustrates us.
We feel unworthy of your love,
   even, sometimes, beyond forgiveness,
   for we go on making the same mistakes,
   day after day,
   week after week,
   year after year.
Yet you assure us,
   through bread and wine,
   that you do not want us to be burdened by guilt
   or crushed by the weight of our many mistakes.
We are reminded in Christ that you want us to feel loved,
   valued and accepted for who we are,
   forgiven and restored,
   set free to celebrate life in all its fullness.
So, then, we come,
   conscious of our weakness,
   acknowledging our faults,
   but, above all, rejoicing in your grace,
   through which we know ourselves to be your people,
   your children,
   chosen and precious in your sight.
Receive our thanks,
   through Jesus Christ our Lord.
Amen.

42
For all the ways we have failed you,
   Lord,
   have mercy.

For all the ways we will fail you again,
   Lord,
   have mercy.

For all the ways we have failed our neighbour,
   Lord,
   have mercy.

For all the ways we have failed our loved ones,
   Lord,
   have mercy.

For all the ways we have failed your Church,
    Lord,
    have mercy.

For all the ways we have failed ourselves,
    Lord,
    have mercy.

We have no claim, Lord, on your goodness,
    no reason to expect forgiveness,
    for in so many ways we let you down,
    but we come, trusting in your unfailing love,
    and asking:
    Lord,
    have mercy.
Amen.

_____ Assurances of forgiveness _____

43

Happy is the one whose wrongdoing is forgiven,
  whose faults are covered.
Happy is the one to whom the Lord ascribes no guilt,
  and in whose spirit there is no pretence.
While I remained silent, my body grew weary with my constant groaning,
  for day and night your hand weighed heavily upon me;
  my strength dried up like sap in the heat of summer.
Then I acknowledged my sin
  and did not conceal my guilt from you.
I said, 'I will confess my disobedience to the Lord',
  and you absolved me from my guilt and sin.
Psalm 32:1-5

44

The Lord is merciful and gracious,
  abounding in steadfast love and not easily riled.
He does not constantly accuse
  or forever nurse his anger,
  nor does he deal with us according to our sins
  or repay us for our mistakes.
His unswerving love towards those that fear him
  is as great as the heavens are high above the earth.
He banishes our faults from us
  as far as the east is from the west.
Psalm 103:8-12

45

No one who conceals mistakes will prosper,
  but whoever confesses and turns from them will obtain mercy.
Proverbs 28:13

46

Jesus said to them,
  'It is not those who are healthy who need a physician
  but those who are sick.'
'I have come not to call the righteous
  but sinners.'
Mark 2:17

47

'Father,
    forgive them,'
    said Jesus,
    'for they do not know what they are doing.'
Luke 24:34

48

'Has no one condemned you?' he asked.
'No one, sir,' she answered.
Then Jesus said, 'I do not condemn you, either.
Off you go, and from now on do not sin again.'
John 8:10-11

49

There is no distinction,
    since all have sinned and fall short of the glory of God.
They are now justified by his grace as a gift,
    through the redemption that is in Christ Jesus.
Romans 3:23-24

50

God showed his love for us in this way:
    that while we were yet estranged from him,
    Christ offered his life for our sakes.
Romans 5:8

51

There is, then, no condemnation now for those in Christ,
    because the law of the life-giving Spirit
    has liberated us from the law of sin and death.
I am convinced that nothing can separate us from Christ's love.
Neither death nor life,
    nor angels nor demons,
    nor the present nor the future,
    nor any powers,
    nor height nor depth,
    nor anything else in all creation
    will ever be able to separate us from the love of God
    that is ours in Christ Jesus our Lord.
Romans 8:1-2, 38-39

52

We have redemption in him through his blood,
  our sins forgiven through the riches of his grace
  that he has so generously heaped upon us.
Ephesians 1:7-8a

53

God forgave us all our sins,
  cancelling the debt written against us in the ledger
  with all its legal requirements,
  irrevocably doing away with it
  by nailing it to the cross.
Colossians 2:13

54

Here are words that you should trust and fully accept:
that 'Jesus Christ came into the world to save sinners'.
1 Timothy 1:15-16

55

If we claim to have no sin,
  we are fooling ourselves
  and the truth has no place in us.
If we confess our sins,
  he is just,
  and we can rely on him to forgive our sins
  and cleanse us from all evil.
1 John 1:8-9

Words of promise
and reassurance

56

We have all gone astray like sheep,
   each going our own way,
   but the Lord has laid on him the offences of us all.
Isaiah 53:6

57

Pay attention, everyone who is thirsty –
   come,
   find water;
   and you that have no food –
   come,
   buy and eat!
Come now,
   and buy wine and milk,
   not for money
   but beyond price.
Why spend your money on what is not bread
   or offer your labour for that which cannot satisfy?
Listen carefully to what I say,
   and you will eat what is good,
   delighting yourselves in the richest of food.
Isaiah 55:1-2

58

Ask
   and it will be given to you;
   seek,
   and you will find;
   knock,
   and the door will be opened.
Matthew 7:7

59

Take my yoke on you
   and learn from me,
   for I am tender and humble in heart

and you will find quietness for your souls –
for my yoke is easy
and my burden is light.
Matthew 11:29-30

60
'Anyone who drinks mere water,'
  said Jesus,
  'will soon be thirsty again,
  but whoever drinks the water I offer will never thirst again,
  for that water will become a bubbling spring,
  welling up within,
  spilling over into eternal life.'
John 4:13-14

61
On the final day at the climax of the Feast,
  Jesus stood and proclaimed for all to hear,
  'If any of you are thirsty
  come to me and drink.
As the Scripture puts it,
  "Streams of living water will flow from the heart of whoever
    believes in me."'
John 7:37-38

62
You will know the truth,
  and the truth will set you free.
John 8:32

63
I have come so that you may have life,
  and live it to the full.
John 10:10

64
We know that all things finally work together for good
  with those who love God,
  having been called according to his purpose.
Romans 8:28

65

When, having given thanks,
   we drink from the cup at the Lord's Supper,
   we are sharing together in the blood of Christ.
Similarly,
   when we break and eat bread,
   we are sharing together in his body.
Just as there is one loaf of bread,
   from which we all share,
   so we,
   though we are many,
   are one body through him.
1 Corinthians 10:16-17

66

We proclaim Christ crucified,
   an offence to the Jews and plain folly to others,
   but to those who have been called,
   whether Jews or otherwise,
   it is the message of Christ,
   the power and wisdom of God.
1 Corinthians 1:23-24

67

Anyone united with Christ is a new creation;
   the old self has passed away in its entirety;
   everything is made new.
2 Corinthians 5:17

68

Praise be to the God and Father of our Lord Jesus Christ,
   by whose inestimable mercy we have been born again
   to a living hope
   through the resurrection of Jesus Christ from the dead,
   to an inheritance that is incorruptible,
   unspoiled
   and unfading.
1 Peter 1:3-4

69

Listen carefully,
   for I stand at the door, knocking.
I will go in and eat with all who hear my voice and open the door,
   and they will eat with me.
Revelation 3:20

Words of institution

70

While they were eating together,
   Jesus took bread,
   blessed and broke it,
   before handing it to his disciples, with the words:
   'Take
   and eat,
   for this is my body.'
Then he took a cup,
   and, after offering thanks,
   he passed it to them, saying,
   'Drink from this,
   each one of you,
   for this is my blood of the new covenant,
   poured out for you and for many,
   to make possible forgiveness for all.'
Matthew 26:26-28

71

During supper, he took bread,
   and, having given thanks,
   he broke it
   and gave it to them, saying,
   'Take this; it is my body.'
Then he took a cup,
   and, giving thanks to God,
   he handed it to them,
   and they all drank from it.
Then he said,
   'This is my blood,
   the blood of the covenant,
   shed for many.
I tell you the truth,
   I will not drink of the fruit of the vine again
   until that day when I drink it fresh with you
   in the kingdom of God.'
Mark 14:22-25

72
When the appointed hour came,
  he and his disciples sat down at the table.
Then he told them,
  'I have yearned to share this Passover meal with you
  before facing the suffering I must go through,
  for I will not eat it again
  until it finds its fulfilment in the kingdom of God.'
Having said this,
  he took a cup,
  and, having given thanks, he said,
  'Take this,
  and share it among you,
  for I will no longer taste the fruit of the vine
  until the kingdom has dawned.'
Luke 22:14-18

73
Taking some bread,
  and thanking God for it,
  he broke it into pieces
  and distributed it among them,
  saying,
  'This is my body,
  given for you;
  do this,
  to remember me.'
Similarly,
  taking a cup after supper,
  he said,
  'This cup,
  poured out for you
  represents the new covenant,
  sealed by my blood.'
Luke 22:19-20

74
Jesus said to them,
  'I am the bread of life;
  no one who comes to me will ever hunger,
  and whoever trusts in me will never thirst.
The Father's will is this:
  that all those who see and believe in the Son
  will enjoy eternal life,
  for I will raise them up on the last day.'
John 6:35, 40

75

'I tell you this,' said Jesus,
    'you do not have life in you
    unless you eat the flesh of the Son of Man
    and drink his blood.
My flesh is true food,
    and my blood true drink.
Those who eat my flesh
    and drink my blood
    possess eternal life
    and at the end of time I will raise them up.
They will live in me,
    and I in them.'
John 6:53-56

76

Our Lord Jesus,
    on the night of his betrayal,
    took bread,
    which, after thanking God for it,
    he broke, saying,
    'This is my body,
    broken for you;
    do this in memory of me.'
Similarly,
    he took a cup afterwards, saying,
    'This cup is the new covenant in my blood;
    whenever you drink it,
    do so in memory of me.'
Whenever you eat this bread
    and drink from this cup,
    you testify to the Lord's death,
    until he comes.
1 Corinthians 11:23-26

Prayers of thanksgiving

77
Lord Jesus Christ,
    we share in this meal not in wistful nostalgia or sombre remembrance
    but joyfully reminding ourselves of the enormity of your love
    and the awesome sacrifice you made on our behalf.
We take bread
    and drink wine
    so that we might never forget all you have done,
    your faithfulness instead staying fresh in our minds,
    colouring each moment of every day.
Lord Jesus,
    whatever else we may fail to do,
    teach us to come in your name
    and to do this, in memory of you.
Amen.

78
Gracious God,
    we come with so many emotions –
    this simple celebration,
    these gifts of bread and wine,
    speaking more powerfully than words alone can ever begin to;
    stirring our hearts
    and kindling our imagination.
We are filled with awe
    and consumed with wonder,
    our spirits soaring to you in joyful worship.
We are overcome with sorrow,
    ashamed at our faults and weakness,
    conscious that we, as much as any,
    were responsible for the agony of your Son on the cross.
Above all, though, we come with thanksgiving,
    marvelling at the extent of your love,
    revelling in your grace revealed through him,
    exulting in your gift of new life and everything that entails –
    peace,
    joy,
    hope,
    purpose,

freedom
and fulfilment.
Gracious God,
gratefully we acknowledge you
not just in words but with thankful lives,
lifting up heart, voice and soul in grateful adoration
for all you are
and all you have done
through Jesus Christ our Lord.
Amen.

79

Lord Jesus Christ,
we thank you that we are here at your invitation,
as your guests,
at your table,
in your house.
You were broken and poured out for us.
No words can thank you enough.

We thank you for this opportunity to meet together:
to share with you and with one another
in this simplest of meals
yet richest of feasts.
You were broken and poured out for us.
No words can thank you enough.

We thank you for all that this sacrament represents:
your willingness to suffer for our sakes
and to sacrifice all,
in order to serve us
and to set us free from sin and death.
You were broken and poured out for us.
No words can thank you enough.

We thank you that we look here to the future
as well as the past,
this meal not a memorial but an act of celebration,
a joyful anticipation of your coming again.
You were broken and poured out for us.
No words can thank you enough.

Lord Jesus Christ,
 gladly and gratefully we come,
 in remembrance of you,
 in recognition of you
 and in response to you.
You were broken and poured out for us.
No words can thank you enough.

Receive our joyful, grateful worship.
Amen.

80
Lord Jesus Christ,
 knowing the cup you would drink from –
 the cup of betrayal and denial,
 suffering and death –
 still you gave thanks to God.
For the wonder of your sacrifice,
 gratefully we respond.

Lord Jesus,
 knowing what was to come –
 your body broken,
 your blood spilled –
 still you gave thanks for bread and wine.
For the wonder of your sacrifice,
 gratefully we respond.

Lord,
 knowing what you have done,
 rejoicing in what you continue to do,
 joyfully we come,
 gladly giving you thanks.
For the wonder of your sacrifice,
 gratefully we respond.
Amen.

81

Lord Jesus Christ,
   for walking the way of humility –
   sharing our humanity,
   entering our world,
   emptying yourself to become the servant of all –
   we gratefully respond.
Such love is too wonderful.
Lord, we thank you.

For walking the way to Jerusalem –
   knowing what it would cost you,
   aware of the hostility of your enemies,
   yet refusing to take an easier path –
   we gratefully respond.
Such love is too wonderful.
Lord, we thank you.

For walking the way of the cross –
   enduring the trauma of Gethsemane
   and the agony of Calvary,
   all to set us free and bring us life –
   we gratefully respond.
Such love is too wonderful.
Lord, we thank you.

For walking the way to Emmaus –
   meeting your followers on the road,
   speaking your living word
   and through bread and wine testifying to your resurrection –
   we gratefully respond.
Such love is too wonderful.
Lord, we thank you.

For walking *our* way –
   matching your stride with ours,
   constantly by our side,
   there to guide, support and bless –
   we gratefully respond.
Such love is too wonderful.
Lord, we thank you.
Amen.

82

Lord Jesus Christ,
 we remember today that you broke bread with the one who was to
  betray you,
 and shared wine with the one who was to deny you,
 enduring anguish in Gethsemane
 and agony on the cross
 for those who in their different ways would fail you in your hour of need.
You gave your life,
 not because any deserved it
 but because nothing could destroy your love or stifle your purpose.
For devotion and mercy beyond our imagining
 we give you heartfelt thanks.

Lord Jesus Christ,
 remembering the anguish and agony you suffered,
 we rejoice today that you invite us in turn to break bread
 and share wine,
 even though we fail you as much as any,
 our faith weak,
 our commitment poor,
 our love flawed
 and our service fitful.
You died for us,
 not because we deserve it
 but because your love is just as sure
 and your purpose just as certain.
For devotion and mercy beyond our imagining
 we give you heartfelt thanks.

Lord,
 we will eat together,
 drink together
 and marvel afresh at all you have done for us,
 at all you continue to do
 and all you will yet do in the days ahead.
Though we do not deserve your goodness
 and can never merit your mercy
 we come with confidence,
 knowing that however much we may fail you,
 you will not fail us.
For devotion and mercy beyond our imagining
 we give you heartfelt thanks.
 Amen.

83

Lord Jesus Christ,
  we remember how, before you broke bread,
  you gave thanks for it.
So now we follow your example,
  giving thanks in turn.

For all that bread meant to the people of Israel –
  symbol of deliverance,
  reminder of Passover –
  Lord,
  we thank you.

For all that bread means to the hungry –
  symbol of sustenance,
  life-giving nourishment –
  Lord,
  we thank you.

For all that bread meant to Jesus –
  symbol of sacrifice,
  token of his broken body –
  Lord,
  we thank you.

Lord Jesus,
  we remember how, before you shared wine,
  you gave thanks again.
So once more we give you thanks.

For all that wine has meant across the centuries,
  symbol of fruitfulness,
  means of celebration,
  Lord,
  we thank you.

For all that wine meant to the Apostles,
  symbol of Christ's blood shed for all,
  sign of new beginnings,
  Lord,
  we thank you.

For all that wine means to the Church,
  symbol of life,
  outpouring of the Holy Spirit,
  Lord,
  we thank you.

Lord Jesus Christ,
   for all this,
   and, above all, for what bread and wine mean to us today,
   symbols of your awesome grace,
   your sacrificial love,
   your daily presence
   and your eternal purpose,
   Lord,
   we thank you.

Hear our prayer,
   for we offer it in remembrance of you.
Amen.

84
Mighty God,
   our discipleship isn't perfect –
   far from it.
We have as many questions as answers,
   as much doubt as faith,
   for there is so much that we do not understand,
   that leaves us troubled and confused.
But we are reminded at this table
   that Jesus died for those whose discipleship was flawed,
   whose faith was imperfect
   and whose understanding was partial.
For giving us so much
   though we offer so little in return,
   Lord, we thank you.

Gracious God,
   our love isn't perfect –
   anything but.
We serve self rather than others,
   putting our own interests before yours,
   for there is so much about loving that frightens us,
   its challenge too daunting to contemplate.
But we are reminded at this table
   that Jesus died for those whose love is limited,
   whose devotion is poor
   and whose worship is weak.
For giving us so much
   though we offer so little in return,
   Lord, we thank you.

Merciful God,
    our lives are not perfect –
    nowhere near it.
We are easily led astray,
    often disobedient;
    so much within us opposed to your guidance,
    so little in tune with your will.
But we are reminded at this table
    that Jesus died for those whose lives are blemished,
    whose service is feeble
    and whose commitment is lacking.
For giving us so much
    though we offer so little in return,
    Lord, we thank you.

Sovereign God,
    gratefully we worship you,
    in the name of Christ.
Amen.

85

Sovereign God,
    we celebrate the message of the gospel proclaimed at this table.

We are reminded here of the triumph of love,
    your victory, through Christ, over violence, hatred and intolerance.
In a world still scarred by these evils
    you promise that love will finally win through.
For that assurance,
    Lord, we thank you.

We are reminded here of the triumph of truth,
    your victory, through Christ, over deceit, corruption and falsehood.
In a world still racked by these evils
    you promise that truth will finally win through.
For that assurance,
    Lord, we thank you.

We are reminded here of the triumph of grace,
    your victory, through Christ, over guilt, sinfulness and rebellion
        against you.
In a world still troubled by these evils
    you promise that grace will finally win through.
For that assurance,
    Lord, we thank you.

We are reminded here of the triumph of life,
    your victory, through Christ, over death, destruction and loss.
In a world still broken by these evils
    you promise that life will finally win through.
For that assurance,
    Lord, we thank you.
Amen.

86
Gracious God,
    for loving us enough to share our humanity –
    born among us,
    walking our earth,
    experiencing our frailty and fears,
    our joys and sorrows –
    in awe and wonder
    we thank you.

For loving us enough to share our death –
    dying on a cross,
    bearing our sins,
    enduring suffering and sorrow,
    darkness and despair –
    in awe and wonder
    we thank you.

For loving us enough to share *your* life –
    life eternal,
    abundant,
    brimming over in all its fullness,
    beyond our finest words or wildest imagining –
    in awe and wonder
    we thank you.

For inviting us to share in bread and wine –
    gratefully remembering,
    eagerly anticipating,
    conscious of all you have done
    and all you have yet to do –
    in awe and wonder
    we thank you.
Amen.

Celebrating the feast

To be used prior to or during the breaking of bread and sharing of wine

87
Bread and wine,
  light and life,
  love and mercy,
  grace and truth.
These are God's gifts,
  offered to you.
Take,
  and rejoice.

88
The broken bread,
  Christ's body,
  beaten,
  bruised,
  broken –
  a sacrifice of love.

The poured-out wine,
  Christ's blood,
  spilled for you,
  given to you,
  flowing through you –
  an offering of grace.

Eat and drink in faith,
  and find nourishment for your souls;
  your hunger met,
  your thirst quenched.
Eat,
  drink,
  and be filled.

89

We break bread,
    remembering the anguish at Gethsemane,
    the agony of the cross,
    the coldness of the tomb,
    the brokenness of the Apostles –
    life extinguished,
    offered freely,
    without reserve –
    his gift to us,
    bought at such cost.

We share wine,
    remembering the faith at Gethsemane,
    the victory of the cross,
    the emptiness of the tomb,
    the joy of the Apostles –
    life restored,
    offered freely,
    without reserve –
    his gift to us,
    beyond price.

We eat,
    and we drink,
    remembering the awfulness
    and the awesomeness
    of this meal:
    the dying
    and the rising;
    the end
    and new beginning.
Christ has died.
Christ has risen.
Let God be praised!
Amen.

90

Eat this bread
    and let the love of God fill you.

Drink this wine
    and let the grace of God engulf you.

91
Broken bread,
  living bread,
  allaying your hunger,
  nourishing your soul.
Eat,
  and be filled.

Poured-out wine,
  new wine,
  quenching your thirst,
  refreshing your spirit.
Drink,
  and be satisfied.

92
Eat this in memory of one who died,
  in honour of one who lives,
  in anticipation of one who will come again.

Drink this,
  recalling the past,
  celebrating the present
  and trusting in God's future.

93
He took bread,
  knowing he would soon be broken:
  such love,
  such devotion,
  offered to you.

He took wine,
  the cup he had begged to be spared:
  such pain,
  such cost,
  borne for you.

94

In the one who was broken for you –
　　who wants to bind up your wounds
　　and send you on your way,
　　restored,
　　renewed –
　　find healing and wholeness.

In the one whose blood was spilled for you –
　　who yearns to help you start again
　　and send you on your way,
　　remade,
　　redeemed –
　　find mercy and love.

In the one who gave his all for you –
　　who longs to turn the water of your life into wine
　　and to send you on your way,
　　revived,
　　rekindled –
　　find joy and peace.

95

The bread of life nourish you,
　　sustain you,
　　strengthen you
　　and build you up.

The new wine of Christ enliven you,
　　uplift you,
　　excite you
　　and course within you.

96

His body was broken –
　　not for the few,
　　the special,
　　the elite,
　　but for you
　　and for many.

His blood was shed –
　　not for the good,

the blameless,
the holy,
but for you
and for many.

Draw near, then, with confidence.
Eat and drink with thanksgiving.
Christ offered his life and offers his love,
   to you
   and to all.

97
A morsel of bread,
   a massive sacrifice.
A sip of wine,
   a fountain of life.

Let the God who brings strength out of weakness,
   plenty out of little,
   the great from the small,
   share your life
   that *you* may share *his*.

98
Take and eat,
   not because you *must*
   but because you *may*;
   because Christ loves you
   and invites you to love him in turn.

Take and drink,
   not because you *ought* to
   but because you *can* do;
   because the Christ who died
   invites you to share his life.

Prayers of intercession

99

Lord Jesus Christ,
  you wrestled in Gethsemane with a turmoil of emotions.
Hear our prayer for all today who wrestle in turn,
  struggling to make sense of life,
  unsure of their ability to get through.
Reach out in love,
  reach out to bless.

After sharing supper you faced betrayal and denial.
Hear our prayer for all today who feel let down by loved ones,
  abandoned by those they looked up to,
  forsaken by people they trusted.
Reach out in love,
  reach out to bless.

You endured mockery and humiliation before Pilate.
Hear our prayer for all today who are misrepresented,
  misjudged and mistreated,
  their humanity belittled,
  their basic rights denied.
Reach out in love,
  reach out to bless.

You suffered unspeakable agony on the cross.
Hear our prayer for victims of violence and torture,
  and for those whose bodies are broken by injury or disease.
Reach out in love,
  reach out to bless.

You entered into the darkness of death and coldness of the tomb.
Hear our prayer for those coping with terminal illness,
  for those we have loved and lost,
  for all who have died.
Reach out in love,
  reach out to bless.

Lord Jesus Christ,
  you rose again,
  all that would deny life and destroy good overcome,
  done away with,
  defeated.

Grant new beginnings in our world today,
   victory over everything that frustrates your purpose,
   and the assurance of your kingdom,
   where sorrow, sickness and suffering will be no more.
Until then we pray,
   reach out in love,
   reach out to bless.
Amen.

100

Jesus Christ,
   Light of the World,
   wherever life seems dark, bleak, hopeless,
   may your love bring a new dawn.
Gracious Saviour,
   hear us.

Jesus Christ,
   Shepherd of the Sheep,
   wherever people feel lost,
   searching for guidance and direction,
   may your love lead them forward.

Jesus Christ,
   Bread of Life,
   wherever people hunger for meaning and purpose,
   something to give shape to their lives,
   may your love nourish them deep within.
Gracious Saviour,
   hear us.

Jesus Christ,
   Living Water,
   where life has lost its sparkle
   and laughter seems a thing of the past,
   may your love rekindle joy.
Gracious Saviour,
   hear us.

Jesus Christ,
   the True Vine,
   wherever your people strive to serve you,

working for your kingdom,
may your love flow in, through and from them.
Gracious Saviour,
    hear us.

Jesus Christ,
    Prince of Peace,
    wherever there is war and division,
    hatred and violence,
    may your love bring lasting reconciliation.
Gracious Saviour,
    hear us.

Jesus Christ,
    Lamb of the World,
    wherever there is hurt and suffering
    may your love bring healing.
Gracious Saviour,
    hear us.

Jesus Christ,
    Man of Sorrows,
    wherever there is heartache and heartbreak
    may your love bring comfort.
Gracious Saviour,
    hear us.

Jesus Christ,
    the Resurrection and the Life,
    wherever death casts its shadow
    may your love bring the promise of eternal blessing.
Gracious Saviour,
    hear us.

Jesus Christ,
    Lord of all,
    to you be praise and glory,
    honour and worship,
    now and always.
Gracious Saviour,
    hear us.
    Amen.

101
Suffering Saviour,
  broken for all,
  we bring to you our fractured world,
  scarred by so many gaping wounds.

We pray for the hungry and homeless –
  victims of famine, disaster, war or oppression,
  denied not just the bare essentials of life
  but also the resources and opportunity to work for change.
Risen Lord,
  bring hope and new beginnings.

We pray for the sick and suffering –
  those wrestling with illness or disease,
  those disabled in mind or body,
  those coming to terms with the prospect of death.
Risen Lord,
  bring hope and new beginnings.

We pray for the sorrowful –
  those hurt or betrayed in relationships,
  those whose dreams have been shattered,
  those mourning loved ones.
Risen Lord,
  bring hope and new beginnings.

We pray for all whose lives have been blighted by evil –
  victims of violence, war and terrorism,
  of crime and corruption,
  of physical, sexual or verbal abuse.
Risen Lord,
  bring hope and new beginnings.

We pray for communities and society as a whole –
  racked by tensions and division,
  torn by prejudice and discrimination,
  disfigured by fear and mistrust.
Risen Lord,
  bring hope and new beginnings.

We pray for this planet you have given us –
  once seeming so solid and secure
  but exposed now as all too vulnerable,
  ravaged by years of plunder and abuse.

Risen Lord,
   bring hope and new beginnings.

Suffering Saviour,
   where we see problems to which there seem no solutions,
   needs to which there seem few answers,
   reach out to bring wholeness and healing,
   the opportunity to learn from the past and so build for the future.
Risen Lord,
   bring hope and new beginnings.

In your name we ask it.
Amen.

102
Gracious Lord,
   reminded of all you suffered for our sakes,
   we bring before you the pain and sorrow so many endure.

We pray for reconciliation in a world of so much division –
   an overcoming of the barriers of fear, hatred and suspicion
   that overshadow so many lives.
Lord Jesus Christ, suffering to bring us life,
   hear our prayer.

We pray for justice in a world of haves and have-nots –
   an end to greed, corruption and exploitation;
   to persecution and oppression;
   to violence and terror;
   to all that denies dignity of life and opportunity for the future.
Lord Jesus Christ, suffering to bring us life,
   hear our prayer.

We pray for unity in the Church –
   a spirit of trust and harmony,
   love and acceptance,
   so that, respecting our differences,
   we may work together as one people
   with one goal.
Lord Jesus Christ, suffering to bring us life,
   hear our prayer.

We pray for those of all faiths, philosophies, creeds and convictions –
   that there may be dialogue rather than confrontation,

and respect rather than dismissal.
Lord Jesus Christ, suffering to bring us life,
     hear our prayer.

We pray finally for those, known and unknown to us,
     stretched to breaking point by their experiences of life –
     the disheartened and disillusioned,
     the depressed, lonely, afraid and anxious,
     the sick and terminally ill,
     those who mourn loved ones;
     all for whom the future seems bleak or the present hopeless.
Lord Jesus Christ, suffering to bring us life,
     hear our prayer.

We ask it in your name.
Amen.

103
For all who have lost faith in love,
     may your dying and rising, Lord, rekindle trust.

For all who have lost faith in truth,
     may your dying and rising, Lord, rekindle trust.

For all who have lost faith in justice,
     may your dying and rising, Lord, rekindle trust.

For all who have lost faith in good,
     may your dying and rising, Lord, rekindle trust.

For all who have lost faith in life,
     may your dying and rising, Lord, rekindle trust.

For all who have lost faith in themselves,
     may your dying and rising, Lord, rekindle trust.

For all who have lost faith in others,
     may your dying and rising, Lord, rekindle trust.

For all who have lost faith in God,
     may your dying and rising, Lord, rekindle trust.

However much faith may be a struggle,
     and however much hope may seem in vain,
     may your dying and rising, Lord, rekindle trust.

In your name we ask it.
Amen.

104

Living God,
    we are reminded as we share this supper
    of how, before he died, Jesus prayed for unity –
    not just in the Church and among Christians
    but in the world as a whole;
    between individuals and nations,
    creeds and cultures.
So now we pray for harmony and peace,
    an end to all that divides.
In a broken world,
    may all be one through Christ.

We pray for those places scarred by violence and conflict,
    sectarian tension or ethnic unrest,
    warfare, terrorism or genocide.
In a broken world,
    may all be one through Christ.

We pray for victims of intolerance and prejudice,
    hatred and persecution;
    all whose lives are blighted by division and discord,
    religious extremism or political ideology.
In a broken world,
    may all be one through Christ.

We pray for those who ferment division,
    inflaming passions and inciting violence,
    resorting to the bomb or bullet in pursuit of their goals,
    maiming or killing the innocent with no compunction or remorse.
Stir their consciences and bring an end to the cycle of violence.
In a broken world,
    may all be one through Christ.

We pray finally for the Church,
    asking forgiveness for its history of disunity
    and praying for an ever-deepening spirit of togetherness,
    so that, instead of denying your purpose,
    it may testify to your reconciling love,
    which breaks down all that keeps us apart.
In a broken world,
    may all be one through Christ.
    Amen.

105
Lord Jesus Christ,
   broken for all,
   risen for all,
   we bring before you the broken people of our world.

We pray for the broken in body:
   victims of disease, hunger or neglect,
   of torture and violence,
   of disaster or accident.
Loving Lord,
   bring healing.

We pray for the broken in mind:
   those oppressed by fears and phobias,
   alcohol or drug abuse,
   depression or other clinical disorders.
Loving Lord,
   bring healing.

We pray for the broken in spirit:
   those whose hopes have been shattered,
   trust betrayed,
   faith destroyed,
   or resilience tested beyond the limit.
Loving Lord,
   bring healing.

Lord Jesus Christ,
   broken for all,
   risen for all,
   grant, we pray, renewed life for all.
Loving Lord,
   bring healing.
Amen.

106
Lord Jesus Christ,
   as you put your faith in God's future,
   trusting that you would drink again of the fruit of the vine
   in your Father's kingdom,
   so we pray for new beginnings in our world today.
Gracious Lord,
   hear us.

May peace replace war,
   dialogue replace confrontation,
   and unity replace division.
Gracious Lord,
   hear us.

May those who grieve find joy,
   those who despair find hope,
   and those who suffer find relief.
Gracious Lord,
   hear us.

May the homeless receive refuge,
   the hungry receive food,
   and the oppressed receive justice.
Gracious Lord,
   hear us.

May truth conquer falsehood,
   love conquer hatred,
   and good conquer evil.
Gracious Lord,
   hear us.

Help all to put their trust in you,
   confident that grace will triumph over law,
   right over wrong,
   and life over death.
Gracious Lord,
   hear us.
Amen.

107
Where life is dark,
   may your presence bring light.

Where evil is strong,
   may good be stronger.

Where suffering destroys,
   may healing restore.

Where sorrow bows down,
   may joy lift up.

Where doubt creeps in,
   may faith hold out.

Where deceit obscures,
   may truth illuminate.

Where hatred divides,
   may love unite.

Where war rages,
   may peace reconcile.

Where death casts its shadow,
   may life shine afresh.

Sovereign God,
   may the victory we celebrate in Christ
   transform not just this but every moment.
Amen.

108
Lord Jesus Christ,
   who endured such anguish in Gethsemane,
   hear our prayer for those who,
   as was so with you,
   wrestle with what the future might bring,
   uncertain of their ability to meet it,
   nervous,
   troubled,
   afraid.
Gracious Saviour,
   be present in their need,
   and lead them safely through.

Lord Jesus Christ,
   falsely arrested, accused, imprisoned and condemned,
   we pray for those who,
   as was so with you,
   are denied their rights,
   wrongfully charged,

cruelly treated
or unfairly judged.
Gracious Saviour,
 be present in their need,
 and lead them safely through.

Lord Jesus Christ,
 flogged, humiliated, nailed to a cross,
 we pray for those who,
 as was so with you,
 are tortured,
 abused,
 victimised,
 despised,
Gracious Saviour,
 be present in their need,
 and lead them safely through.

Lord Jesus Christ,
 bearing our sins in awful isolation,
 we pray for those who,
 as was so with you,
 feel hopeless,
 abandoned,
 crushed,
 alone,
Gracious Saviour,
 be present in their need,
 and lead them safely through.

Lord Jesus Christ,
 laid in the coldness of a tomb,
 we pray for those who,
 as was so with you,
 face death
 or who have passed from this life,
 their earthly journey near its close
 or at an end.
Gracious Saviour,
 be present in their need,
 and lead them safely through.

Lord Jesus Christ,
 our Lord,
 we pray for ourselves and all people, that,

as was so with you,
we may enter into the joy of your kingdom,
the beauty of your presence,
celebrating your new creation,
and rejoicing in your love for evermore.
Gracious Saviour,
be present in *our* need,
and lead *us* safely through.
Amen.

Words of acclamation
and celebration

109
The one who died is risen!
The one bowed down is lifted up!
The one nailed to a cross is enthroned on high!
The one who gave his all is Lord of all.
Hallelujah!
Hallelujah!

110
He was broken to bring us healing,
   crushed to set us free,
   killed so that we might truly live.
But he is alive,
   risen,
   victorious;
   the King of kings
   and Lord of lords!
To God be praise,
   now and always!
Amen.

111
The cross was empty,
   the body cut down
   and the tomb sealed.
It was dark.
The tomb was empty,
   the body gone,
   the stone rolled away.
It is light!

112
Whatever life may bring,
   whatever you are facing,
   do not lose hope,
   for the risen Christ is here,
   speaking his word,
   giving his promise:
   'Peace be with you . . .
   do not be afraid . . .
   for I will be with you to the end of time.'

113
In the garden, love continued to burn.
After darkness, light continued to shine.
To the broken, grace continues to flow.
From the tomb, life continues to blossom.
To the One who died,
   is risen
   and will come again,
   be praise and glory,
   honour and worship,
   now and for evermore!
Amen.

114
The day was over,
   the dream destroyed,
   life seeming at an end.
Until a stranger met Mary in the garden
   and pilgrims on the Emmaus Road;
   until the Lord appeared to his Apostles,
   alive,
   victorious;
   until the truth dawned that the journey was not finished,
   but only just begun!

Words of dismissal

115

Listen!
What do you hear?
The thud of nails shattering flesh and bone.
The sound of wood creaking under its load.
The gasp of a man, hanging there in agony.
The Lord is speaking:
   'Father, forgive them.'
   'Why have you forsaken me?'
   'It is finished!'

The dream is dead,
   the body cut down.
It is dark.

Listen again!
What do you hear?
The sound of women weeping in the garden.
Shouts of confusion.
Cries of disbelief.
The Lord is speaking:
   'Fear not.'
   'It is I.'
   'See my hands and my feet.'

The dream lives,
   the Lord is risen!
A new day is dawning.

Go now
   in the light of the living Lord
   and let his life flow in you
   and through you,
   now and always.
Amen.

116
Evil has done its worst –
   poisoning,
   perverting –
   but good is not defeated.

Hatred has done its worst –
   wounding,
   wronging –
   but love is not exhausted.

Violence has done its worst –
   bullying,
   breaking –
   but peace is not destroyed.

Darkness has done its worst –
   obscuring,
   oppressing –
   but light is not extinguished.

Death has done its worst –
   destroying,
   denying –
   but life is not vanquished.

Defeat is turned to victory,
   despair to hope,
   doubt to faith –
   for it was not the end but a new beginning.

Go, then, in that confidence, to serve the Lord,
   knowing that nothing is finally able to thwart his purpose,
   and no one is beyond his grace.
May all things praise him.
Amen.

117
The Christ who bids you, 'Come',
   now bids you, 'Go.'
As you are loved,
   love in turn.
As he has served,
   serve in turn.

As he forgives,
   forgive in turn.
As he stays true,
   stay true in turn.
The Christ who bids you, 'Go',
   goes with you.
Walk then with him
   until your journey's end.

118
His body was broken . . .
   for you.
His blood was shed . . .
   for you.
Bread has been shared,
   wine poured out . . .
   for you.
Go now,
   keep the faith,
   serve others,
   strive after good,
   love all . . .
   for *him.*

119
We have eaten bread
   and drunk wine,
   but the meal is not over,
   for Jesus offers us bread of life,
   living water,
   food for our souls,
   a cup running over with new wine.
Celebrate his gift,
   rejoice in his love,
   and live each day to the full
   until that time when we will feast with him
   in his Father's kingdom,
   and taste the blessings yet in store,
   for all eternity.

120

What's done is done –
   a sacrifice made,
   the price paid,
   redemption and new life won for us in Christ.

What's done is done –
   the past is history,
   our mistakes are put behind us;
   here and now, a new day begins.

What's done is done,
   and cannot be undone!
Go, then, in faith –
   the Lord has set you free!

121

No more wrestling with guilt,
   no more burden of failure,
   no longer captives of the past,
   no longer troubled by the future.
The victory is won,
   mercy is assured,
   evil and death are defeated,
   life is yours.
Go then, and live it,
   rejoicing in the love of Christ
   and serving him as best you can,
   by his grace.

122

After tears came laughter,
   after darkness, light;
   after doubt came faith,
   after despair, hope;
   after fear came confidence,
   after confusion, certainty;
   after ends came beginnings,
   after death, life.

The meal is ended,
 but the journey is not over,
 for after worship comes service,
 after blessing, response.
Christ is waiting:
 walk with him
 and he will walk with you.

123

As you have received,
 go now to give.
As you have been nourished,
 go now to nurture.
As you have celebrated God's love for you,
 go now and show love to others.
As you have remembered the broken Christ,
 go now and walk the way of sacrificial service.
As you have worshipped the risen Christ,
 go now and live each day with joy,
  to his glory.

124

The meal was over,
 the table was cleared,
 and they went out . . .
 to face the anguish of Gethsemane,
 the horror of the cross.
Jesus Christ,
 even in our darkest moments,
 the bleakest interludes of life,
 go with us.

The meal was over,
 bread broken and shared,
 and they went out . . .
 their eyes opened,
 their hearts singing within them.
It was the brightest of dawns.
Jesus Christ
 as we end our worship,
 and return to the daily round of life,
 go with us.

The meal is over,
   and we go out in turn.
Help us to walk each moment,
   whatever it might bring,
   with your love in our hearts,
   your word on our lips,
   your truth in our thoughts
   and your grace in our deeds.
In all of life, Lord,
   go with us.

Blessings

125

The Lord who feeds us so faithfully,
   blesses us so richly,
   leads us so surely,
   forgives us so freely,
   supports us so staunchly
   and loves us so completely,
   go with us now and always.
Amen.

126

The Christ who died for you,
   live in you.
The Christ who loves you,
   shine through you.
The Christ who welcomes you,
   go with you,
   now and always.
Amen.

127

May the love of Christ shine in your eyes,
   the compassion of Christ work through your hands,
   the word of Christ fall from your lips
   and the life of Christ flow through your veins,
   to his glory.
Amen.

128

Lord Jesus Christ,
   may the new wine you so freely offer
   sparkle within us,
   course through our veins
   and flow out to others.
Amen.

129
Loving God,
   may the bread of life always nourish us,
   living water daily refresh us,
   the broken Christ constantly inspire us
   and the risen Lord unceasingly guide us.
Amen.

130
Lord Jesus Christ,
   as you have served,
   may we serve in turn;
   as you have loved,
   may we love in turn;
   as you have cared,
   may we care in turn;
   as you have lived,
   may we live in turn;
   until that day we are one with you
   and with all your people,
   and you are all in all.
Amen.

131
Living God,
   though we will always fall short,
   may something of Christ live within us:
   the faith with which he faced doubt in Gethsemane,
   the humility with which he faced mockery before Herod,
   the courage with which he faced agony on the cross,
   the love with which he faced hatred from his enemies,
   and the mercy with which he responded to those who took his life.
May a little of these gifts be found in us,
   so that we may honour you more completely
   and work more effectively for your kingdom.
Amen.

132
Lord,
   be in our loving
   and in our living;
   be in our speaking

and in our serving;
be in our working
and in our resting;
be in our dying
and in our rising.
Living Lord,
   be all in all.
Amen.

133
Bread of Life,
   meet our needs.
Broken Christ,
   heal our wounds.
Suffering Saviour,
   show us mercy.
Living Lord,
   give us life.
Amen.

134
May the broken Christ,
   the poured-out Christ,
   strengthen us in body,
   enrich us in mind
   and nurture us in spirit.
Amen.

135
The source of life go with you
   as you celebrate all he has given.
The pattern of life guide you
   as you walk in his way.
The giver of life sustain you
   as you offer him your service.
The resurrection and the life bless and keep you,
   now and for all eternity.
Amen.

136
Day by day, O God,
    may the living Christ speak *to* us,
    grow *in* us,
    work *through* us,
    shine *from* us
    and dwell *with* us.
Amen.

137
Living God,
    may love continue to fill us
    and grace continue to thrill us,
    as we return to the daily business of life.
Teach us to give without reserve,
    as you have so freely given to us,
    so that the ordinary may be touched by the divine,
    each moment consecrated to you
    and sanctified by your touch.
In the name of Christ we ask it.
Amen.

138
To him who bore our sorrows to win us joy,
    who took on darkness to bring us light,
    who was broken to make us whole
    and who endured death to secure us life,
    be praise and glory,
    honour and adulation,
    now and for evermore.
Amen.

139
Lord Jesus of Bethlehem,
    be born in us.
Lord Jesus of Galilee,
    speak to us.
Lord Jesus of Gethsemane,
    strengthen us in times of trial.

Lord Jesus of Calvary,
    support us, even in suffering and death.
Lord Jesus of the empty tomb,
    grant us life in all its fullness.
Lord of heaven and earth,
    may our lives bring honour to your name,
    now and always.
Amen.

Also by Nick Fawcett

Short Prayers for Public Worship
1500566   1 84417 016 0

These short prayers, designed to be read aloud in acts of worship, express the ups and downs on the journey of discipleship, ring out in praise and thanksgiving to God for what he has done, and focus intercessions on issues personal and global. Prayers cover times of day, seasons of the Christian year and big issues like peace, evil and the kingdom of God, as well as more personal themes like strength in weakness, hope and despair, guidance, and relationships. A resource of over 550 prayers for use in church, or in groups, and written so that those leading can pray from the heart in straight-forward, everyday language.

Selected Prayers for Public Worship
1500586   1 84417 070 5

This resource of 500 selected prayers, written by Nick Fawcett and designed to be read aloud in acts of worship, expresses the ups and downs on the journey of discipleship, rings out in praise and thanksgiving to God for what he has done, and focuses intercessions on issues personal and global.

Prayers cover times of day, seasons of the Christian year and big issues such as peace, evil, and the kingdom of God, as well as more personal themes like strength in weakness, hope and despair, guidance and relationships.